P9-BAT-497

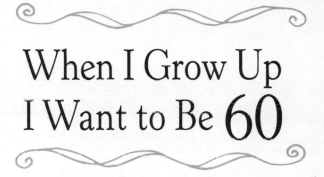

# When I Grow Up
# I Want to Be 60

Most Perigee Books are available at special quantity discounts for bulk purchases for sales promotions, premiums, fund-raising, or educational use. Special books, or book excerpts, can also be created to fit specific needs.

For details, write: Special Markets, The Berkley Publishing Group, 375 Hudson Street, New York, New York 10014.

# When I Grow Up
# I Want to Be 60

## Wendy Reid Crisp

A Perigee Book

**A Perigee Book**
**Published by the Penguin Group**
**Penguin Group (USA) Inc.**
**375 Hudson Street, New York, New York 10014, USA**
Penguin Group (Canada), 90 Eglinton Avenue East, Suite 700, Toronto, Ontario M4P 2Y3, Canada
(a division of Pearson Penguin Canada Inc.)
Penguin Books Ltd., 80 Strand, London WC2R 0RL, England
Penguin Group Ireland, 25 St. Stephen's Green, Dublin 2, Ireland (a division of Penguin Books Ltd.)
Penguin Group (Australia), 250 Camberwell Road, Camberwell, Victoria 3124, Australia
(a division of Pearson Australia Group Pty. Ltd.)
Penguin Books India Pvt. Ltd., 11 Community Centre, Panchsheel Park, New Delhi—110 017, India
Penguin Group (NZ), Cnr. Airborne and Rosedale Roads, Albany, Auckland 1310, New Zealand
(a division of Pearson New Zealand Ltd.)
Penguin Books (South Africa) (Pty.) Ltd., 24 Sturdee Avenue, Rosebank, Johannesburg 2196,
South Africa

Penguin Books Ltd., Registered Offices: 80 Strand, London WC2R 0RL, England

Copyright © 2005 by Wendy Reid Crisp
Text design by Tiffany Estreicher
Cover design by Charles Björklund
Cover art by Eliza DeVille
Interior illustration by Ben Gibson

All rights reserved. No part of this book may be reproduced, scanned, or distributed in any printed or
electronic form without permission. Please do not participate in or encourage piracy of copyrighted
materials in violation of the author's rights. Purchase only authorized editions.

PRINTING HISTORY
Perigee hardcover edition / April 2006
ISBN: 0-399-53105-X

PERIGEE is a registered trademark of Penguin Group (USA) Inc.
The "P" design is a trademark belonging to Penguin Group (USA) Inc.

This book has been cataloged by the Library of Congress

PRINTED IN THE UNITED STATES OF AMERICA

10   9   8   7   6   5   4   3   2   1

*to the memory of*
*Jennifer Moyer,*
*who left everything*
*better than she found it*

# Thank you

Lari Shea, Maureen Crawford, Patty Friedmann, Harriett Foster, Nancy Kaytis-Slocum, Susan Fales, Ruth Anne Stretch, Ginger Lourenzo, Sue Schiller, Elaina Zuker, Catherine Mace, Sue Laris, Willa Briggs, Barbara Carroll, Beverley Eastwood, Darlene Ricotta, Patricia Westfall, Suzannah Mellon, Cheryl Etter, Linda Moreland, Ruth Bass-Green, Ann Barbata, Karen Pingitore, Dee Johnson, Pam Mauney, Jody Fleury, Ann Coopersmith, Talia Carner, Sara Matta, Helaine Shilling, Giuliana Halasz, Jeanne DuPrau, Lynette Matyshock, Sally Dolfini, Eva Eng, Caroline Blattner, Jill Mason, Trudy Banks, Marlene Nunnemaker, and the two Johns: editor Duff, and husband Lestina.

# Foreword

Whoops. We've hit the "S" word. Sixty. A Speed bump, the first one I've noticed. *Don't tell me to slow down. If I alter the course, that will be my decision.* A Sexagenarian and still a Smarty-pants. Hmm. What other "S" words define us and inspire us? I asked each woman whose voice is in this book to think of such a word (or make one up)—an "S" word that describes her feelings or ambitions for this era of our lives. The women who responded are Asian Americans, Middle Easterners, Caucasians, Latinas, Native Americans, and African Americans; they are from across the United States, as well as from China, Venezuela, Mexico, Canada, Scotland, Indonesia, and Israel. Some of them have been married to the same man for forty years; some have been married many times; some are divorced, some are gay; some are single by choice, some are widows. The group includes mothers and grandmothers and (two) great-grandmothers; there are women who have not had children, women who have adopted children, women who have lost children. The voices are those of teachers, from preschool to graduate school; a neonatal nurse; two social workers; a bookseller; four writers and a poet; an anthropologist; a banker; mortgage brokers, real estate brokers, and stockbrokers; homemakers; an artist; a potter; an equestrienne; a pianist; a historian; a city planner; shopkeepers; entrepreneurs; and a postmaster. Remarkably, about half of the women represented here have at least one parent living—a statistic that is unique in modern history.

Several of the women are survivors of breast cancer; one has bone cancer. Some have had family members who struggled with Alzheimer's; a few report they have been active in substance abuse recovery programs.

All of us who speak on these pages came of age in the late 1960s; we protested the war in Vietnam, marched for civil rights, lived in communes; the women's movement challenged us, threatened us, involved us, and inspired us. Some of us jumped on the career carousel in navy-blue suits and red bow ties and went for the brass ring; others walked a more traditional path, sneaking off only occasionally to participate in networking receptions, sensitivity sessions, or consciousness-raising groups.

Years before our secrets became the public fodder of television talk shows, we began to trust in each other and to confide. We learned then that our differences are valuable, even honorable; we celebrate them as they bind us together and mourn when they divide us.

For whatever our differences, we are a historical cohort: We are the most populous group of women

to attain this age, and, relative to our foremothers, we are affluent, educated, healthy, independent, and still burning with the heat of the fire that forged us. We are Sixty. We are Strong. Hear us roar.

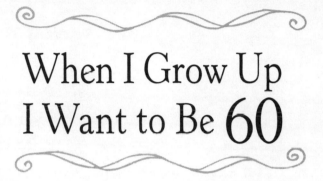

# When I Grow Up
# I Want to Be 60

# Introduction

My mother said, "*Never* say 'never'," and I went right ahead and said it anyway, often several times a day, and now I've rounded a corner and found myself staring down my *nevers*.

Ten years ago, I wrote *100 Things I'm Not Going to Do Now That I'm Over 50*. The old Yiddish warning "If you want to hear God laugh, make plans," comes to mind, as does "If you want to see God double over with hysteria, publish your New Year's resolutions." On thirty-seven "things," I've done a one-eighty. I wrote, for example, in rash mid-century confidence, that I was no longer going to lecture the young (does volunteering at the elementary school count?), or sleep on wrinkled sheets (*right*; I'm hauling out the mangle iron as we speak).

Ten years ago, I foresaw a serene, manageable future. "What could be more chaotic than the past?" I said, proving that naivete endureth forever. And then, I married, divorced, and remarried in the space of three years; hosted two radio shows; wrote 260,000 words worth of newspaper columns; edited a magazine; made money and lost money; became a grandmother; studied Spanish, bridge, rose gardening, and documentary filmmaking; hiked fifteen miles in a single day to pick huckleberries; decorated a retro condo; was awarded prizes in photography; put up a thousand jars of fruit; preached sermons; won a four-wheeler; and moved seven times in six years to and from four states, including a surprising relocation to the Minnesota prairie.

Even as recently as my mid-fifties, I laughed and said, "I still don't know what I want to be when I

grow up." Well, ready or not, I have grown up, and
I know what I want to be. It's what I am: Grateful.

Wendy Reid Crisp
Ferndale, California
January 2006

Over 60, all grown up, and now we are . . .

# Shape-shifters.

Last fall I telephoned Julie, and her husband an-
swered. "She's not home right now," he said.
 "She's in the Amazon."

Some people have us fixed in such form-fitting personalities, they are rattled by the tiniest aberration in our behavior. "When did you learn how to arrange flowers?" my mother asked suspiciously, as if the act of reading about *ikebana* and assembling hydrangeas was evidence of a double life.

*When I surprise my husband and my father—they have one hundred years of combined knowledge of me—they shake their heads, amazed; the looks on their faces are priceless. Shocking the rest of the world is easier, but not as satisfying. —Cathi*

Over 60, all grown up, and now we are . . .

# Sharpshooters.

"Let the boys win," said my third-grade teacher. "It's important to them. And don't show off. No one will like you." We were Special Forces in smocked dresses, walking softly, carrying our intelligence as concealed weapons. Eventually, we were unmasked—it's stressful for a ten-year-old to pretend to forget what a planet is or purposefully misspell *foreign*. Sadly, however, our third-grade teacher was right, and never more so than when we entered the business world. Feminist movement or not, smart women—and there are so many of us!—make people nervous. As well we should. The weapon is no longer concealed—and at sixty, we fire at will.

"You should always look smart," my aunt said, but she meant nothing about brains and everything about wearing a navy-blue-and-gray suit with a hat and white gloves.

❧

*I'm smart about everything I say and do. It's a revelation that, as it says in Proverbs, brings "sweetness to the soul and healing to the body." I have lived long enough to experience life's trials. I have survived breast mastectomy and reconstruction; good and bad marriages; good and bad friends. Now I can trust my instincts and the voice inside that says it's okay to be me, to live to the fullest, to my heart's desire.* —Ruth

# Starting over.

My first car was a '51 Ford. At night, I parked it on an incline. To get the pistons firing, I had to put it in second gear, depress the clutch, release the emergency brake, roll down the hill, and pop the clutch. Bingo. Maybe if I end each day on a mountaintop, I can roll out of bed in the morning, release the brakes of fear and confusion, and jolt that old engine into joy.

What would be the ratio of mileage to human years? About 4,000 miles per year? If so, I've got 244,000 miles on me. I rotate my tires, get regular tune-ups, and occasionally replace the windshield. I'm holding my breath that the transmission will last.

*Sixty?! No way. I'm setting back my odometer.*

*—Alice*

Over 60, all grown up, and now we are . . .

# Sisters.

We ignore the dated stereotypes, the ones that separate us into the women who went to Woodstock and the women who didn't; the ones who backpacked across India and the ones who day-camped at Swope Park. The years have worked a strange magic: The hippie is a stockbroker, the PTA president felts in a yurt in Uzbekistan, the corporate vice president stays home and baby-sits her grandchildren.

There is but one circle to complete, and complete it we must, no matter where on the circumference we started.

*In sisterhood there is celebration. We celebrate our lives, ourselves, each other—sometimes with belly laughs, sometimes with teary eyes. Always with true sorority.* —Ann

Over 60, all grown up, and now we are . . .

# Subversive.

Reasoning, compromising, consulting the bylaws, waiting for a green light from the national office—what a charming, civilized way to fritter away our time. In the meantime, please refer all desperate acts of compassion to the appropriate committee. We'll get back to you.

Doing the right thing is almost always a revolutionary act.

❧

*What to do? Something, anything. One voice, one candle, one small step. And no one can tell me what to do. I know what to do. I don't always do it, but I know what to do.* —Connie

Over 60, all grown up, and now we are . . .

# Skilled.

We storyboarded ad campaigns, kept house, planned museum benefits, sewed Halloween costumes, catalogued phanerogams—and we did it over and over until we thought we were going out of our minds, and then we emerged from the chrysalis of practical education and discovered that we were experts. We can make a Caesar salad—the right way, from scratch—while simultaneously plotting a political campaign. We can direct a choir that sings so beautifully it takes our own breath away. We know how to rig sails and spin wool and vaccinate heifers. And yet we have time for new seductions: Come, learn Urdu, master the butterfly stroke, research botanicals in Antarctica, design a wedding dress.

We have survivor skills. We are the strong links in the community chain. In the mirror is the face of our mother, in our heart is the courage of our great-grandmother.

*As many skills as I have acquired, there are many more I want. Three examples: I'd like to be an expert on my computer and all things web-related. I want to learn the names of the gorgeous succulents on my balcony. I want to learn—and be able to perform—the yoga asanas.* —*Michaela*

Over 60, all grown up, and now we are . . .

# Sexy.

A strappy sandal dangled from a long leg, showing off perfect hot-pink toenails. "Wow!" I said. "Gorgeous. And your toes match your poncho."

"Yes," she said. "And under the poncho I have no breasts. My feet are the new 'Why don't you come up and see me sometime?'"

Youth is not wasted on the young. But sex is.

❧

*My last cancer checkup came back clear. Whew. The only problem now is with bone density. I had to get off all estrogen which, along with age, has taken its toll on my spine. With the meds, I have to start an exercise program, which is not my style; going to a gym, aargh. Of course, I don't smoke, I don't drink alcohol, and I avoid fried foods—all of which I thought was saintly enough. What does that leave for fun? See above.*

*—Maureen*

# Scandalous.

There's no percentage in being a sixty-year-old good girl. If you're still trying to please your parents—for love or for the inheritance—God bless you, but the rest of us are ditching the bake sale and checking into the day spa for salt rubs.

The curtain is rising on the third act, and if there hasn't been much of a plot yet, you've lost your audience. Follow the music. If you're unsung, sing; if you're un-flung, fling.

*I have moved into a rich, savory life: spicy dancing—salsa, flamenco, tango; spicy romance on nude mid-night swims in Latin lagoons; a spicy dress and a hot, spicy rum drink on a mountaintop in Brazil on a starry night . . . and amor, amor, amor.* —Dee

Over 60, all grown up, and now we are . . .

# Surrendering.

Power struggles bloody both sides. Go for the guillotine win, or walk away.

"Did you just quit?" I was asked when I left a job that had become unpleasantly political.

"No," I said. "I didn't 'just' quit. I *quit*. Quit is an honorable option."

❧

*I have become strategic. I choose my battles carefully. Since I seldom enter the fray, when I do, watch out.*

*—Vivian*

Over 60, all grown up, and now we are . . .

# Small-town socializing.

Who could have predicted that retirement would bring us, clueless, to an uncatered world in constant need of macaroni salad for two hundred?

## The Rules of Community Potlucks

1. "Bring a dish to share" means food for twelve servings.

2. Buy utensils, hotpads, and trivets at the dollar store and expect to lose them.

3. Don't display the chicken in a family heirloom and then hover over the platter in a nervous frenzy.

4. Prepare recognizable food. No one wants to wonder if it's chicken or rattlesnake.

5. Comment not. The donor of the marshmallow-covered baked beans is standing directly behind you.

6. If you're competitive, keep in mind: Italian food goes first.

*Unless graciously offered to you, don't go home with anyone else's leftovers. Ha! You could say that's my philosophy of life.* —Frances

Over 60, all grown up, and now we are . . .

# Stumbling.

Overnight, a silent, destructive, alien commando unit has built uneven curbs and short steps; from out of nowhere, I am attacked by doorknobs and end tables, a rock, a measuring cup, and a low-slung cupboard.

I used to worry about dying in a plane crash or as the victim of some tabloidesque crime. Now I envision another scenario: I will catch a billowing sleeve on the handle of a French door, stumble over a braided rug, and pitch headlong into the andirons. "How did she die?" people will ask, and my friends will say, "Big blouse."

❧

*Don't worry, it may never happen. —Gail's coffee cup*

# Social butterflies.

Television destroyed visiting. Folks used to drop by after dinner, and the adults shared the news and played pedro or 500 or spades or Pit or Milles Bornes or pinochle or canasta or Parcheesi while the children played upstairs or outside or in the barn. When those adults moved into RV parks and retirement villages and nursing homes, they made new friends because they knew how to play games. What will be our vestigial social skill? Remembering all the words to "Blowin' in the Wind"?

The most powerful antidepressant just may be the rush of dropping the queen of spades on someone else's trick.

*My mother is 99, and she lives near me in an assisted-living facility. She's healthy, and she has a sense of humor—most of which she directs at her awareness that she has no memory. No memory, that is, of anything except dominoes. I have never been able to beat her in dominoes.*　　　　　*—Bev*

Over 60, all grown up, and now we are . . .

# Swift.

Exquisite freedom was the theme of our childhood fantasies—the wild girl in the forest, the artist hidden in the attic, the girl who could talk to animals. "She can run like the wind." Curled up in overstuffed chairs, snuggled with flashlights under the covers, we read of their visions, their adventures. We will be like that, too, we promised; we will fly away into the night.

The girl's voice is strong within me. She has been there all along, it seems, waiting out the noisy clamor of growing up.

*On my sixtieth birthday, I competed in a fifty-mile endurance race on horseback through a virgin redwood forest. On my fiftieth birthday, I won the event. This time, riding a less experienced horse, I didn't go for the win. My goals were to beat the trail and complete the race with my horse in good condition. Instead, I won! My two kids rode with me, as they did in the best years of their childhood, when the woods rang with shouts of "Wait for Mommy!" as I followed them down the trails.* —Lari

# Simple.

Peg Bracken, in *I Hate to Housekeep*, advised young housewives to begin each daily cleaning in a different room. Otherwise, she warned, we will continually tire out in the same spot, until one day we'll have to saw off the back bedroom. Cleaning house, simplifying life—same thing. Tackle a different problem every day. By the time we've completed a circle of concerns, half of them no longer exist, and a heartening number will have been solved by someone else.

Whenever you hear yourself say, "It's more complicated than that," remember: No, it's not.

∞

*I want to be simple—not the slobbering on your shirt, I-can't-remember-where-I-put-my-keys simple—but the simple that is uncomplicated, unafraid, uncluttered, and transparent: emotionally, spiritually, and musically. I want to be happy, playful, surrounded by real people and silly animals. I've grown out of the complicated "intellectual" questions that stealthily put a wall around me for so many years. I embrace the change.* —Sue S.

Over 60, all grown up, and now we are . . .

# Salmon sharers.

A languid summer of backpacking and fishing in Oregon came to an abrupt halt when my romantic companion caught a forty-two-pound Chinook and gave me half to put in my freezer. I hosted a grand dinner party. He dumped me. "You're bizarre," he said. "What kind of a woman would give away a man's fish?"

Being sixty means never having to apologize for our idiosyncrasies. It's the contemporary version of *I'm OK, You're OK*. It's called "I'm Crazy, You're Crazy, So What?"

*One man's bizarre is another man's wife.*

*—A suggested epitaph*

Over 60, all grown up, and now we are . . .

# Sick.

Why does my dog have better medical insurance than I do?

We adopted Frank from the pound. His $9-a-month in-surance covers prescriptions, X-rays, surgeries, hospi-talization, ultrasounds, CAT scans (no puns accepted), homeopathic treatments including acupuncture and chiropractic, chemo, and referrals. Frank may select the veterinarian of his choice. Clearly, it's time to register with the pet insurance company as, say, Princess Fifi, and go to the veterinarian when I'm under the weather. I asked our local vet, "Any downside to this idea?"

"If you were to stay over following surgery," Dr. Sil-ver said, "you might find the accommodations a bit spare. We give you a pad and a big blankie, but you would be lying on cement, with no TV and no ad-justable bed. You'd be in a private room, though—we only have private rooms. I don't think the food would be that much different from hospital food." Meow.

❧

*I want to be schnauzerly, like Sadie, setting paw to the pavement, yapping at will—then moving on, guilt-free.*
                                                              —*Cheryl*

Over 60, all grown up, and now we are . . .

# Swamped.

I had a list. It was composed of end-
less dreams and plans—personal,
creative projects I would complete when
I no longer had an eight-to-seven job. No one
warned me about the cosmic catch-22: *There was
already a volunteer-accounts-payable list out there
with my name on it.*

The fact that we grasshoppers who never bothered to put anything "aside" will have to work until heavenly shades of night are falling does not deter the rest of the world from demanding that we, at last, shoulder community duties. ("Hey, *we* carried the ball during your career days—now, we're going fishing. *You* raise the money for the repertory theater and drive old Mrs. Putney to the eye specialist. Consider it payback for the three million miles of car-pooling you avoided because you worked in the city.")

*I am hoping retirement will be as free as were my first twenty years. My work is done. There is no more pressure to support my husband's ambition and my children's dreams; my parents are no longer living. Won't this be the time when I can finally pursue my own ambitions, my own dreams, and my own needs?* —Jody

Over 60, all grown up, and now we are . . .

# Stuffed.

How—*why*—did I acquire five generations of photographs and letters, piles of books, CDs, videos; drawers jammed with sentimental clothing ("Don't throw out my soccer T-shirts!"), and an attic crammed with furniture, games, and tools?

I am not the curator of the Museum of Me. I am a pioneer, entering the frontier of the New Sixties. Best to travel light.

❧

*I'm sending all the family heirlooms to someone who enjoys dusting.* —Harriett

# Sensual.

We attended conferences and listened to motivational speakers tell us to believe in ourselves, pamper ourselves, and go for the gold. Trouble is, reality requires triage: When you're going for the gold—or even the silver—while trying to believe in yourself when all about you are unbelievers, the pamper part doesn't always make the cut.

Our bodies are orchestras, the members of which have been playing together for over sixty years. Even with the loss of a bassoon or a trumpet or two, our music is soothing and stirring. Sensuality is the warm-up.

My aunt is eighty-seven. After her official retirement, she was too bored to "hang around with the girls, have lunch and play cards," so she volunteered at the tour office of the Jewish Seniors Activity Center. Last summer, at lunch at her apartment on a very hot day, I gave her three rose-shaped, lavender-scented floating candles. I told her how I use candles for my bath. The next morning she called. "Last night, I ran a bubble bath, turned out the lights, lit the candles, and put on music. I must have stayed in that bath for half an hour—as if I were in a trance. Then, with the lights still out, the candles burning, and the music playing, I got out of the bath and danced, naked, in my living room! I can't believe I've never done this for myself before."         —Elaina

# Slippery.

Now you see her, now you don't. The heroines in romantic literature mysteriously appear and disappear; the queen masquerades as a pastry chef, the woman barefoot on the beach is glimpsed in the back of the cathedral. We can go anywhere, do anything, be anyone—within the space of an hour or two, if we so choose. Stopping by the casino on your way home from volunteering at the soup kitchen? Ain't nobody's business if you do.

Rip the labels from the lining of your soul. Now you know her; now you don't.

*It seems as if, for my whole life, others have defined who I am. "You are so dependable." "You're always on time." "You're conservative." "You're liberal." "You're a hard worker." "You're lazy." Well, from now on, with that deliciously smooth, soapy feeling of newly shaved legs, I'm slipping out from under labels.*

*—Catherine*

# Sad.

I feel no guilt for grieving for my dog. Yes, there are significant catastrophes, human tragedies that call into question the priorities of mourning the passing of an old pet. Still, Viola was thoughtful, patient, gracious, and loyal—qualities that deserve respectful attention wherever and in whomever we encounter them.

I know . . . loss is the inevitable consequence of living long and loving well. But still, could it be postponed? Not today. Please, not today.

⁓

*I love so many people, so many animals, so many plants even, I've become a walking weep machine.*
—*Jeanette*

# Sure-souled.

I aspire to ethical consistency: Walk the talk, put my money where my mouth is, be a woman of unchanging virtue. Instead, I rant against the exploitation of children in the sweatshops of developing nations as I stock up on $5 bras from Burma.

What we believe, and what we do about what we believe is all we have to offer and all we are expected to give.

*I want to be Santa.*
*Come sit in my lap sweet, small, starving, unsmiling*
*    children, all of you.*
*My reach is long enough, my heart is large enough to*
*    hold you. And I have the time.*
*We won't need to check a list or gaze toward a*
*    camera.*
*Your eager parents will not need to remind you of*
*    what you want.*
*My elves have been busy. The sleigh is packed with*
*    food, water, clothing, and medicine.*
*It may take more than one night to reach you, but I*
*    will reach you.*
*I'm Santa.*                                    *—Ruth S*

Over 60, all grown up, and now we are . . .

# Step-grandmothers.

And if, for any reason, we actually *use* this title, may our voices cackle and our noses grow long and warty. "Here, my pretty, have a bite of this shiny red apple." Stepgrandchildren? Please.

The devoted caregiver of an aged uncle was the daughter of his son's former live-in. Like a mountain stream, the natural course of love meanders.

*Who will take care of me when I am truly old? I look around at the potential candidates, and I begin to understand "You reap what you sow." Yikes.* —Liz

# Serene.

Why are so many elderly women angry? Where do they come from, the rage junkies, high on this cheap, contagious, addictive source of adrenaline? Spare me from the pushers of hate, and spare me from my own weakness that tempts me to treat the blues with a red shot of anger.

The evils in this world—regardless of the cyclone of fury generated—are not centered in she who immersed the congregation's eighty-cup coffeemaker in the dishwater. The evils in this world are war, famine, pestilence, and plague—the same old four guys and the people who ride with them.

Serenity is a side effect of wisdom.　　　　— Diana

51

# Scuba diving in Sulawesi.

On the bulletin board by my desk is a sepia-toned postcard of four matronly women and one young man. The women are dressed in black; the man, wearing a loose white shirt and pants, holds the reins of one of the camels on which the women are seated. In the background is a pyramid. I don't recall how I came to be in possession of the photo. What I do know is, those pre–World War I women are my heroes. Not only have they traveled far from home without escorts, they have climbed atop camels in the desert while wearing huge, feathered hats and twenty pounds of bustled dresses.

On the back of the photograph, a note, written in elegant Palmer penmanship, reads: HERE WE ARE IN EGYPT. ANOTHER ADVENTURE. NEXT TIME, WE HOPE YOU WILL JOIN US. FONDLY, MARGARET. Sign me up, Maggie. In this world, or the next.

∞

*I have recently returned from Papua New Guinea, and the trident-shaped island of Sulawesi in Indonesia. Age will never stop me from diving in remote tropical ocean waters; it is a unique experience of freedom, beauty, and adventure.* —Ann C.

# Sibyl.

How did I deduce, when he bought the yellow shirt, that he was having an affair? How could I have known, just by talking to the interior decorator for the corporate offices, that the company was nearing bankruptcy? What vision came to me and revealed that the neighbors were drug smugglers? Prophetesses we are. Oracles. If, by sixty, we've made enough mistakes, divine insight is handed out for free.

Time has made fools of us all.

*I'm a seer, so my daughter says. I see, all right. I see her making the same mistakes I did.* —Sharon

Over 60, all grown up, and now we are . . .

# Spectacular.

Ego is good. Our demons lurk in our insecurities.

We can do many things, it's true. But there are things we will never do. We won't have the money or the opportunity; we won't have enough talent or enough dedication. If we insist on making a "lack list," we will find it is infinite. *Shhh.* Don't awaken the genii of jealousy.

〜

*I'm not making any lists. It's too difficult to type with a large cat on the lap. What was the question?*

*—Trudy*

# Satisfied.

I said, "I did the best I could," and as soon as I said it, I knew it wasn't true. I'm certain my great report card in the sky has the notation, DOES NOT WORK UP TO POTENTIAL. But I did the best I could at doing the best I could. Does that count?

All routes ennoble, all routes humble—and, in four-score years, all routes converge. One day, we lift up our eyes from the road less traveled and discover ourselves in bumper-to-bumper traffic.

❧

*When I turned sixty, I felt old, as if my life were almost over. I examined each choice I'd made along the way and wondered if I could have done something more important. Gradually, I realized that what I had chosen—to raise, with my husband, four children to become honest, kind, and hardworking—was very important. It was exactly what I was supposed to have done. I don't have a pension, but I do have a home, a family, friends, health, a busy world of interests, and delightful grandchildren. I am satisfied, with my life and with my age, and I thank God for that.* —Ginger

Over 60, all grown up, and now we are . . .

# Shui'd. Feng and otherwise.

Doctors and therapists should be required to learn the principles of interior design. Before taking a pill or spending six months at the gym or quitting a job and entering a monastery—first move the furniture and color the walls. Peace of mind? You have no idea.

The original message from the doomsayers was, by the way: "The end of the world is at hand. Re*paint*."

❦

*There is only one rule for home decorating: Everywhere we look, we should see something that makes us happy.* —Hazel

# Strong.

At twenty, we demanded physical independence; at thirty, we grasped emotional independence; at forty, we fought for financial independence; at fifty, we declared social and creative independence. At sixty, whether or not we've declared anything, we *are* independent. It is a gift: We confront and embrace our need for love, support, respect, and acceptance, as we simultaneously love, support, respect, accept—and forgive—others. Therein is the paradox. The source of our strength is our weakness.

I used to be hurt by what people said about me: "She's a bulldozer, a ballbuster; she eats glass." Now I hear, "She's a rock; she'll go to bat for you; she's not afraid of anyone." Apparently, the more you resemble a bull-dozer, the less threatening you are.

*I hate it when people call me strong. "Oh, she's so strong." I feel as if they are negating my journey, the lifetime of work I've done to discover what feeds my soul—resources that include my faith, and individuals among my family and friends who have helped me navigate my way through tough times. If I've become strong, it's because I'm always seeking strength. Don't call me strong— call me resilient.      —Linda R.*

# On Sabbatical.

Biological science tells us that over a period of seven years, all the cells in our body are replaced. If we blend math with maturation—and why not?— we can track our life stages: zero to six, seven to thirteen, fourteen to twenty, twenty-one to twenty-seven, etc. Sixty is in the middle of our ninth life cycle, a cycle that began at fifty-six and will end at sixty-two. For women like me, who tidy by categories, this concept is calming. Every seven years, we tie up a few loose ends, take a year off, and resurface in a new persona.

A life cycle is not a *bicycle*: We don't have to push it to make it go; if we fall off, we don't have to get back on if we don't want to; and sometimes, when we forget how to do something, the knowledge doesn't come back to us and we don't care.

❧

*I will be a spoke—and not the cog. Last summer, in Canada, I experienced our first empty-nest vacation. I had dreaded the passing of the chaos; I found I loved the quiet. I had no idea how much I had been the cruise director: The one who scheduled the meals for twenty-five—and who cooked them—who planned the out-ings, who made the reservations. Instead, last summer, I read and I napped. I went on walks without asking who else wanted to go. I bought a package of salami at Costco, and it was our protein for seven meals. I was liberated by cured meat.* —Sally

# Surprised.

Who would have foreseen that twenty-year-old men, obsessed with (in second, third, and fourth place) software, music, and philosophy, would be the most interesting buddies? "Everyone here probably thinks you're my mother," said my brilliant, straggly-bearded new best friend.

"No, Don," I said, "I don't think so. I'm too old to be your mother."

The continual surprise is discovering that events that seemingly occurred only five years ago actually took place in 1981.

∽◦

*I want to be surprised to my core. Give me that rush . . . when one of my novels is listed on the* New York Times *bestseller list or I am invited to the Academy Awards ceremony, where I'll walk down the red carpet a star. My life will be a party of surprises—and I'll be the one throwing it.* —Talia

# Speechless.

Outraged at a perceived slight to my authority, I ranted to my ninety-one-year-old mother. "How old were you," I cried, "before people started taking you seriously?"

She looked at me—baffled—and said, "About what?"

More than once, I've had the stuffing knocked out of me by someone who said something so off-the-wall it brought me to my senses. Is that what "sensible" means? To survive absurdity? If so, bring it on. I miss Gracie Allen.

*"Whatever you do," I said, "don't throw me a surprise party." They didn't. What a helluva time to start taking me seriously.* —Leanne

# Spontaneous.

I was tutoring a young man in English when he wrote in his notebook, "December is my wedding. I want you to come." I wrote, "Okay." I did not consider whether there would be money enough or time off; I did not worry about whether my husband wanted to go. I did not ask where we would stay. I did not fret, *It's Christmas; we have to be here for the church, for the family.* Instead, I went online and purchased two tickets for a one-month trip to Oaxaca. "That's a pretty long vacation," my husband said anxiously.

"Don't think of it as a long vacation," I said. "Think of it as a very short retirement."

Pondering has its place, but we exert far too much effort on weighing options, consulting budgets, and coordinating schedules. We really aren't that important in the Great Galactic Schematic. ("Sorry I didn't get back to you sooner. I've been in Mexico for a month." "My gosh, has it been a month already?!")

*Spontaneity is the fountain of youth. I don't make long-range plans or worry about what has yet to happen. That's a waste of energy and causes premature wrinkles.* —Karen

# Stoned.

I met an acquaintance in the pharmacy. She said, "I'm buying drugs. We're getting stoned. Gall stoned." We're in the Stone Age, all right—stone broke, stone deaf, millstones, milestones, tombstones . . . just thinking about it gives me the munchies.

In an artsy import shop in Portland I bought a long cotton dress imprinted with turtles. On a very hot day, I wore it instead of shorts (the wearing of which, for me, has been ruled a felony). "Hey," said my cousin, "isn't that a granny dress?"

"Yes, Tad. Everything I wear is a granny dress—and speaking of Cooper, he has four teeth now. Here, wait, I have new pictures."

❧

*Part of me still doesn't trust anyone over thirty. Particularly as that is now the age of my children.*

*—Leslie*

# Same as always.

My uncle was the editor and the photographer of a country weekly newspaper. The focus of most of his photographs—even if the purported subject was a town celebration or the county's welcome of the governor—was me. Hundreds of pictures documented every nuance of my personality. Who I am now—it's all there, right down to the irritable cynic. See? Second from the right in the Jeffersonian ballgown? The scowling little face under the powdered wig?

We know we have an inner child. What we may have forgotten is that when we were children, we had an inner adult.

∾

*Until my dad died at the age of eighty-three, he often said that, inside, he still thought he was eighteen. The Buddhists say the body is merely a vehicle to allow us to reenter this world, to accomplish whatever it is we're going to accomplish here. Part of the reason aging is so shocking is because it's so out of sync with our young, vibrant, interior selves.* —Jill

# Stubborn.

I'm not talking about your great-aunt's cut-off-your-nose-to-spite-your-face stubborn—our stubborn has political and spiritual components. We no longer fear expulsion, jail, unemployment, or disinheritance. There is, as Yeats wrote, a "terrible beauty" in standing fast, and we are beautiful, here, tonight, our wrinkles softened in the glow of the vigil's candlelight.

I've edited my beliefs down to a precious, passionate few, and to those hallowed opinions I hold tight, my fingers entwined about them, a desperate child clinging to the leg of her mother.

*I want to be someone like Eleanor Roosevelt*

*I've spent years wishing this mousy brown hair*
*Now brillo gray covered with blond*
*Would be her lovely silver.*
*That my ordinary face would be filled with her*
    *radiant love.*
*That my demeanor would have her decorum.*
*Most of all I have wished*
*I might emulate her wisdom and activism*
*To make a difference in this world.*

—*Willa*

# Sleepless.

What is that pain behind my ear? Why is my finger swollen? I think I was bitten by that earwig in the artichokes. Quick! Google the symptoms. That's it, I'm dead. Help me clean the house. You can't host a wake in this mess.

The "window of sleepability" opens every ninety minutes. Get up, read a book, check your e-mail, put a load in the dryer, write a poem, play online bridge with that kid from New Zealand, or eat the rest of the spinach lasagna. Insomnia is our body's way of telling us there is something better to do than lie here and—yes, *you do*—snore.

I don't sleep at night. At night, I have hours of delicious solitude. I sleep in the afternoons. Deteriorating daylight, that's what I call afternoons.    —Louise

Over 60, all grown up, and now we are . . .

# Streamlining.

Isn't it curious that as we accumulate more money and rack up the assets to ensure our late-life comfort, we reminisce more and more about those carefree, happy days when we had nothing but two plates and a dented kettle?

A wedding was held in our backyard. An hour before the ceremony, hysteria broke out. The red and white balloons—hung on a post to alert guests that they had reached our obscured driveway—were the *wrong colors*. The bride's colors were lavender and silver. *This ruins everything.*

"Take down the balloons," I said. "If some people get lost, well, maybe they aren't *meant* to be here." I managed a meaningful, *Outer Limits* sort of expression.

It worked. My remark was so weird, the young people regrouped, forgot the balloons, and got married.

Priorities can't be argued; they must be demonstrated.

*Why did I have to reach sixty to learn the value of simplifying? Now someone else can clean for me—I no longer have to have the house perfect and polished. Marie Callender can provide delicious frozen meals (albeit high in fat). My appearance? A bit of blush, eyebrows, lipstick, and I'm good to go. And clothing! Comfy jeans, t-shirts or sweatshirts, Reeboks or Birkenstocks. Life is less stressful and so much more enjoyable.*

*—Linda M.*

Over 60, all grown up, and now we are . . .

# Soaring.

Exercise, chocolate, laughter, and
making love: four delicious
sources of endorphins.
Take two and call me in
the morning.

Lift up your eyes. This suggestion is found so often throughout the Bible one might begin to wonder if it could be, you know, *important*. Lift up your eyes. Just because it sounds poetic doesn't mean it doesn't work.

∾

*My daughter painted a poster and hung it in her bedroom opposite her bed, so it was the first thing she saw when she woke up in the morning. On the poster, a rainbow arched over the words "The sky is the limit." She died of cancer when she was sixteen. Later, when I took the poster down, I thought how often I had said those words. Now I had to believe them. I'd been a mother and a 4-H instructor. I became the administrator of an accounting firm (very firm!), and then, when I turned fifty, I changed careers to study—and master—creative professional portrait photography. Over sixty, I am once again looking up and forward toward the unknown. The sky is the limit . . . as long as we don't do things the way we've always done them.*
*—Marlene*

Over 60, all grown up, and now we are . . .

# Sandwiched.

Remarkably, the decline of my parents and the ascent of my grandchildren have resulted in an unexpected nexus: They all seem the same age—and all much younger than I. I am the only fogey.

A friend was talking about her eighty-nine-year-old mother and her not-yet-three-year-old granddaughter. "Katy is talking clearer and clearer; Mom is more and more difficult to understand. Katy is dressing herself; Mom has to have someone dress her. Katy is getting out of pull up diapers; Mom is getting into them. And they both need me."

<hr>

*The only sight more frightening than watching my sixteen-year-old grandson back out of the driveway is watching my ninety-year-old father pull in.* —Corinne

# Stiff.

As in bored stiff. As in, *Who are these people and what am I doing here?* Once, I would have stayed anyway because I wanted people to like me, even if I didn't like them. That neurosis has been cured by a nine o'clock bedtime.

I demand to be fully engaged. My tolerance level for the mediocre and the dull is near zero. More and more often, when I hear, "Well, that was a waste of time," I am aware of how little time we have to waste.

*And how about feeling just plain stiff? I wake up in the morning, and my body is frozen. I have to lie there and thaw. I want to be supple.* —Helaine

Over 60, all grown up, and now we are . . .

# Selective.

What do we cling to? What will we release? Other women in other times jettisoned grand pianos on the banks of raging rivers and marble-topped breakfronts at the base of the Rockies. What do I carry in my heart that should have been abandoned on the prairies of the past?

When a dear friend, gesturing wildly as she recounted the breakup of her last romance, knocked my great-grandfather's Staffordshire dog off the shelf and onto the flagstone, I knew: It was the dog's time to go.

❧

*Sharing is what I select. Sharing is what keeps me looking forward to sixty-five, seventy, eighty, ninety. I want to share laughter, hugs (especially from grandchildren), chocolate cake, good books, funny e-mails; I want to share my days with friends and with my husband, the love of my life. I want to share adventures, great wines, and singing.* —Suzannah

Over 60, all grown up, and now we are . . .

# Svelte. Suave. Savvy.

Ah, those intimidating "sv" words, the Myrna Loys of vocabulary, so sophisticated, so alluring, so handy on a triple-letter score.

I had been petite (short and small) all my life. I could eat a mountain of food and still fit a size four. Then one day an enchanted mist swept over me and if I even uttered the word *fettucine,* my buttons popped.

❧

*Skinny. That's what I want to be. The night I attend my weekly Weight Watchers meeting without fantasizing about my next meal will be an event to celebrate. Of course, celebrating will mean scarfing down a large piece of cheesecake and a white chocolate candy bar. Or, how about a piece of white chocolate cheesecake washed down with a Diet Coke and a little lime? Oh, well. I'll have skinny to look forward to at seventy.*

—*Lynette*

# Snippy.

I opened my mouth to make a few meaningless re-
marks, and a toad jumped out—an ugly, unkind,
gratuitous sentence that hopped out of sight and
into the ether. I called 911. "I have an emergency
here," I said. "My soul has been invaded by a
wicked crone."

She's still there. That's her, grumbling, putting groceries away, and muttering threats under her breath; I hear her twist a concern—"How is he?"—into a judgment—"This was an accident waiting to happen."

❧

*I still don't know when to shut my mouth. I find both feet stuck in it far too often. My goal for my sixties? To see the big truck barreling down the road before I verbally step in front of it.* —Carly

# Self-assured.

A couple of years ago, I had a vivid dream of my late aunt. I shared the experience with my mother. "She was giving me instructions about maintaining the garden," I said. "She didn't seem to understand that she'd passed away."

"They never do," said my mother. She was folding clothes, and her rhythm of smoothing and tucking didn't miss a beat. "They're always telling me what to do: my sisters, my mother, my father, your father. I don't pay any attention to them. They're dead. What do they know?"

I do, indeed, have miles to go before I sleep. Bossy, demanding ghosts? Only recently have I developed enough self-confidence to deal with the living.

*I accommodated everyone. I would listen attentively and be aware of my body language. I concentrated on my responses so that the other person, whether a friend, a family member, or a client, would feel my acceptance, my suspension of judgment. At social events, I was concerned that everyone have fun; I believed it was my responsibility to see that they did. No surprise, I was constantly anxious, exhausted, and unable to enjoy the moment.*

*Finally, I know what needs to be done, and that knowledge comes naturally. I relate to the world just as I am, as myself.* —Giuliana

Over 60, all grown up, and now we are . . .

# Salt and pepper.

Wise and spicy, smart and sassy—oh, what metaphors are available for the changing color of our hair. As Shakespeare might have written, "Methinks the lady doth euphemize too much."

Nothing is black and white. We have to learn to be comfortable making decisions in a vast gray area— much of which is on the top of our heads.

*Stunningly silver; now that would be elegant. Instead, my muddy brown hair looks like floodwaters filled with gray chunks of driftwood.* —Heidi

Over 60, all grown up, and now we are . . .

# Subdued.

Once we were the life of the party; our stories were the funniest, the most touching, the most outrageous. Today, we share our stories in writings, in song, in paintings, in photographs; somewhat reluctantly, we have relinquished the live stage to younger people who are living new stories and telling them, wonderfully, for confession, reassurance, and affirmation. As we did.

I maintain my dignity only at public events. Our group of women, laughing uproariously and crying without notice, can no longer have "little dinners" in restaurants—we are too disruptive. Someone has to volunteer her place. Someone has to love us enough to vacuum.

*I fear being the buffoon, the one who talks on and on, not noticing glazed-over eyes or hearing the jingling of keys in someone's pocket. I remember too clearly the grown-ups who behaved that way when we were young, and I shudder to think I've become one of them.*                                            *—Marianne*

Over 60, all grown up, and now we are . . .

# Spring chickens.

When my mother was only eighty-nine, she often said, "I wish I were young again." At last, I asked, "What do you mean 'young'? What age do you wish you were?"

"Sixty," she said.

"Sixty!" I said. "What's so great about sixty?"

"Sixty was wonderful," she said. "You kids were gone, we had more money for ourselves, we were healthy, we didn't have to work so hard, and we had lots of friends. Those were the best years of our lives."

When I feel creaky and useless, I go with my mother to the senior lunch and sit at a table filled with elegant, bright women who graduated from high school during FDR's first term. They regard me as someone who just fell off the turnip truck, and I have to remind them that I am a member of the last generation to even know what a turnip truck is.

*Two years before she died, my mother announced that she did not want to be the mother of two old women, and she offered us each $18,000 for a face-lift. My sister was afraid of a general anesthetic; I took the money. So, at least when I'm standing next to my sister, I'm a spring chicken.* —*Patty*

Over 60, all grown up, and now we are . . .

# Stout.

*"Bulky in figure,"* reads the dictionary, followed by *"bold, brave, and dauntless."* Do I get a choice? If it's all or nothing, give me the whole package. I'll settle for being broad in the beam as long as there's beam in the broad.

Stouthearted women, "strong of will and back," abound in history. Here's an account of a mid-1930s fund-raiser in Yampa, Colorado: *"These twenty-three staunch women were equal to the Herculean task of transforming [an old building] into a library. They . . . raised money by giving dances and raffling off cedar chests filled with their own hand work. . . ."* From black-tie benefits at the Waldorf to spaghetti dinners at the Grange Hall, didn't we do this just last week? And yet, the rousing all-male voices in operetta revivals, singing Oscar Hammerstein's lyrics, plead only for "stout-hearted *men*." I guess they know wherein they lack.

❧

*Sturdy is what I want to be. I want legs that will hold me up for travels to interesting spots, and a back that won't get tired when I work in the garden, and hands that can still play the piano, and a heart that will keep going at a nice steady rate for a good long time. I want to keep on doing all those things that I need to be sturdy to do.* —Jeannie

Over 60, all grown up, and now we are . . .

# Safe.

We post–World War II girl babies drew the roller-coaster ticket. We came of age doing our own thing, being cool, protesting, hanging out; we were the token women; we climbed the corporate ladder, made partner, juggled, invested, divorced, cohabited, adopted, remodeled, relocated, and regrouped. The ride isn't over . . . but now we wear seat belts.

Safety is not the absence of danger; safety is the management of fear.

*I live in a remote spot of the country where a wild river meets the sea. I married late—the most wonderful man in the world, and I love that I'm here, in this snug place, with our pets and my garden, looking back on the crazy things I did when I was young, thankful I'll never be doing them again, thankful I survived.* —Nancy

# Selfish.

What a scary concept. Resurrects the angst of adolescence in all its gangly glory; we still cringe from the criticisms. *You are the most selfish person in the world.* Often, this indictment referred to slipping out on a kitchen full of dirty dishes or wanting a new prom dress. *It wasn't fair.* But it's fair now! I will go to a movie by myself, without inviting anyone even though I can think of at least three people who are lonely and bored and I should invite them, but I don't, because I want to see what I want to see, think what I want to think, and pig out on popcorn drenched in ersatz butter without apologizing.

My aunt believed that I should be able to do anything I wanted whenever I wanted. "Poor little lambie," she'd say, watching me write a term paper. "You shouldn't have to work so hard." Her whisper drifts across the years and coddles me when I'm meeting a deadline or cleaning the bathroom or cooking the third meal in six hours for a crowd of ten. "You shouldn't have to wait on all these people. Poor little lambie."

*I've been a chronic do-gooder. Sixty promises freedom—and what is the freedom I crave the most? To be single-mindedly, brazenly selfish, even if only for a few hours a month. I've earned it.* —Sara

Over 60, all grown up, and now we are . . .

# Scrappy.

What is it? Increased testosterone? No more walking miles around the mountain—metaphorically or literally—to avoid a confrontation. I'm almost at the point of hurtling all five-foot-three of me at a burly stranger and saying, "Whaddaya lookin' at, frogface?"

Career counselors have cautioned us to be "assertive, not aggressive." Good advice for a thirty-year-old. Ridiculous at sixty. If we don't seize the moment—and the power—the planet is doomed.

❧

*I'm giving up my childhood belief in Thumper's advice: "If you can't say something nice, don't say nothin' at all." At this age, Dr. Seuss is my sage. As he wrote, "Now my troubles are going to have troubles with me."*
*—Susan F.*

# Sole proprietors.

The root of *retirement* means "to withdraw." If we're talking money, *withdraw* is my favorite word. Otherwise, forget it. I did my withdrawing at ninth-grade sock hops, sitting awkward and alone along the wall. I'm dancing now, with or without an invitation.

In our second—and third and fourth—careers, success is measured in equal ratios of cash, stress, and joy.

❧

*After faithfully fulfilling the roles of daughter, wife, and mother, I'm focused on accomplishing my dream—to commercially produce food products based on long-treasured family recipes. I've become self-determined.*

*—Pam*

# Single.

We didn't plan it this way—or maybe we did. Maybe one day we stopped looking, or stopped longing, and realized that while it would be comforting to have someone to hug, it was equally comforting to leave the light on until the last chapter, to blast Joe Cocker throughout the house, or to leave for London without a filibuster.

Some of us are so ornery we can't even maintain split personalities.

❦

*I like men. I like to be with them. And I have no trouble with commitment. But I'm a late bloomer, now divorced, and I'm just coming into my own with knowing myself. I spent many years trying to please men. The time for matrimony is over. Two fifteen-year marriages ought to be enough.*                    —Sue

Over 60, all grown up, and now we are . . .

# Significant.

As our experiences ripen in the cauldron of our philosophies, our actions become distinctive. We are women of consequence.

Not sure you're significant? Open the envelope that shouts, "You may have already won!" Inside you'll find a note from a young woman that reads, "I want to be you when I am old." We are the role models. Problem is, we secretly believe we're still the age of our protégés.

❧

*Older people are often viscerally dismissed by the young. I intend for my presence to be strong and essential; I will not be considered insignificant.* —Bonnie

# Sober.

Someone said "If it feels good, do it," at the very instant when that was what we wanted to hear, and some people kept doing it, long after it didn't feel good. By sixty, the call to recovery may be the last train to Clarksville.

All of us see through a glass darkly. But it needn't be the bottom of the glass.

✑

*I had my last drink in 1981, right after my fortieth birthday. I'd been to a bon voyage party for a woman whose forthcoming trip I envied; I left and slept with a man I hardly knew and didn't even like. The familiar downward spiral: a bad feeling, booze to make it go away, self-loathing, self-destruction, even more self-loathing. Life "with the lights on" these past twenty-four years has been sweet and exciting, sad and boring—many things, but always clear. There are no clouds in my mind, my brain, or my heart. Sure, bad stuff happens, but I can usually handle it. And when I can't . . . well, there's always peanut M&Ms.   —E.*

Over 60, all grown up, and now we are . . .

# Silk screeners.

Tole painters, photographers. Darlene is writing and illustrating a children's book. Michelle is formulating organic cosmetics. Fran is selling her savory sauces. We have new ideas to express and a new urgency for our expressions to endure.

I won a gargantuan purple ribbon imprinted with EX-HIBITOR OF THE YEAR: HUMBOLDT COUNTY FAIR. It hangs in my kitchen. The big ribbon represents fistfuls of smaller blue and red ribbons I received for photography, preserves, and flower arrangements; it also represents a welcome affirmation. Yes, it announces, you can master new crafts, you can continue to creatively explore the earth's abundance.

∞

*For my fifty-ninth birthday, I held a "last shall be first" event—the "last" for the last year of my sixth decade and the "first" for my first art show. I'd spent the summer painting—twenty-one paintings in a single summer! Now people have purchased my work—I'm sell-a-brating. I had become sour, tired. Writing, and teaching writing, had begun to pale. Now I've begun an art journal. Painting has renewed the writer in me.*

*—Patricia*

# Silly.

In the supermarket, I made goofy faces at the toddler who was slung over his mother's shoulder. He giggled and made a goofy face back at me. I giggled. His mother turned around and smiled. I smiled. "What a sweet little boy," I said, my face composed into a mask of dignified older woman. As they walked out, he shot me another conspiratorial expression. Secret friends in the land of the silly.

As children, we were warned not to be "silly little girls." The message from adults was that silly was the dreaded opposite of serious, and if we wanted to be respected grown-ups we had better learn to be serious. In retrospect, I think they meant stuffy.

❧

*I am loving my second childhood. Unlike the years when I was raising my own three kids, I am completely uninhibited with my grandchildren—I don't give a damn about how silly I look, dancing wildly in the center of the living room, singing, "The wheels on the bus go 'round and 'round."* —Barbara

# Singing.

"Do you sing?" I asked my husband, John, when we were courting. "Only in my heart," he said. A lovely line, but, as it turned out, not true. He sings in the shower, all about the house, in the yard, and, with enthusiasm, in church. It was there I learned the awesome, powerful intimacy of standing together, side by side, singing—not with great voices, but with great feeling.

There are no lyrics more beautiful than the stories in our souls and no music more stirring than that which sets them free.

❦

*I was born in Toyshan, Canton, China, during World War II. My father left China and went to America. My mother stayed with us until, because of so much torture due to the Communist Cultural Revolution, she disappeared. We children were left alone for one year. I was the oldest; I was six years old. I took care of my two siblings until one day, a neighbor helped us to escape to Hong Kong. There, we found our mother. Nineteen years later, we immigrated to America, to San Francisco. My childhood was full of fear. Now I am free of fear. I don't care anymore about what people think, because I have earned my choices. I am not going to argue with anyone, because I have learned that we all have to follow our own learning path. Now I am singing my heart out, praising God and celebrating the enrichment of the years—good and bad—that I have experienced.* —Eva

# Sanguine.

Death is not what scares me. What scares me is someone else writing my obituary.

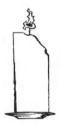

Unless we write our own obituaries, our legacies will be defined by young family members who, while (we hope) are wracked with grief, nevertheless will have to hire a caterer for the wake, meet with the attorney, and ask Betty if she can sing "I'll Fly Away" at the services. Our life stories will be rush jobs reporting that our greatest joys were reading, gardening, and visiting our grand-children, the obit writers. Ryan will submit the picture he took last week when they had you propped up in bed. Lisa won't allow the mention of your first two hus-bands. And no one will recall that you once won the No-bel Prize in physics.

◦———◦

*I don't care what anyone says about me when I'm dead. Except for you-know-what. And that week in Wilkes-Barre. The school deal, I wouldn't want anyone to re-member that, either. Oh, and it's unnecessary to include the cop in Corpus Christi; nobody wants to read those kinds of stories. Other than that, I don't care what any-one says but I've found this photo from 1978. Pretty cute, don't you think? Other than that . . .* —W.R.C.